Help Me Be Good

Fighting

Joy Berry

Illustrated by Bartholomew

Joy Berry Books
New York

This book is about T. J. and his sister, Tami.

Reading about T. J. and Tami can help you understand and deal with fighting.

Sometimes people get angry and want to fight. When people fight, they can hurt each other's bodies.

They can hurt each other's feelings.

They can damage or destroy each other's belongings and things around them.

Never do anything to hurt yourself
or another person.

Do not hit, kick, bite, pinch, or pull
anyone's hair.

Never damage or destroy things.

Do not hit, kick, or throw things that
can be broken or ruined.

Try to avoid fighting. Stay away from people who always make you angry.

Try to avoid fighting. Do not play too roughly. Someone usually gets hurt when people play roughly. The person who is hurt may get angry and want to fight.

Try to avoid fighting. Do not spend too much time with one person. People often fight when they get tired of being around each other.

Ask your parent or someone else to help you if you and the other person cannot decide what to do.

Listen to the person's advice, and then follow it.

You can solve the problems you have with other people without fighting.

If someone does something that makes you angry, do not do anything right away. You might get into a fight if you act too quickly.

Slowly count to ten when you are angry, to give yourself time to calm down.

When you are calm, talk with the person who made you angry. Do not scream. Do not say mean things.

Talk about how you feel. Explain why you are angry. Tell the person what you think should be done.

Give the other person a chance to talk.
Listen carefully. Show respect for the
other person's thoughts and feelings.
Try to understand the other person's
point of view.

Decide what to do about the problem after you and the other person have said what needs to be said. There are at least three ways to solve a problem.

- You can do what the other person wants to do.

- The other person can do what you want to do.

- You both can give in some without giving in completely. This is called compromising.

Ask your parent or someone else to help you if you and the other person cannot decide what to do.

Listen to the person's advice, and then follow it.

Fighting can be harmful. When you fight, you might hurt yourself or others. You might damage or destroy something.

That is why you should not fight.

It is best for everyone when problems are solved without fighting.

Joy Berry Enterprises
146 West 29th St., Suite 11RW
New York, NY 10001

Cover Design & Art Direction: John Bellaud
Cover Illustration & Art Production: Geoff Glisson

Publication Location: HX Printing, Guangzhou, China
Date of Production: February 2010
Cohort: Batch 1

Printed in China
ISBN 978-1-60577-135-9